CLASSIC *f*M

Christmas Favourites

A selection of traditional carols arranged for piano with lyrics

FABER *ff* MUSIC

Contents

Arranged by John Kember and Richard Harris

Faber Music in association with Classic FM, a Global Radio station.
Faber Music is the exclusive print publisher for all Global Radio sheet music product.

© 2010 Faber Music Ltd
First published in 2010 by Faber Music Ltd
Bloomsbury House 74–77 Great Russell Street London WC1B 3DA
Music processed by Jeanne Roberts
Introduction by Julian Haylock
Printed in England by Caligraving Ltd
All rights reserved

ISBN 10: 0-571-53480-5
EAN 13: 978-0-571-53480-7

To buy Faber Music/Global Radio publications, or to find out about the full range of titles available,
please contact your local retailer, or go to www.fabermusic.com or www.classicfm.com/shop.
For sales enquiries, contact Faber Music at sales@fabermusic.com or tel: +44 (0)1279 828982.

Foreword

Christmas without the sound of carols would be unthinkable, and as they have developed over hundreds of years, their melodies have come to evoke tranquility and peace. Playing these joyful arrangements of carols is an excellent way of bringing a festive atmosphere into your home.

My favourites are 'While Shepherds Watched', 'O Little Town of Bethlehem', and 'Once In Royal David's City'.

These are pieces that inspire hope, and I wish you the best of luck with learning them.

John Brunning, Classic FM

Hear these carols on the Classic FM Full Works Album 'Carols from King's' (CFMFW095) available exclusively from HMV

Introduction

Although the source of many traditional carols is sadly lost in the mists of time, some of the most popular can be safely assigned to their original composers. **Once in Royal David's City** is the most famous melody by Henry John Gauntlett (1806-1876), the composer of over 100 hymns, who played the organ in the premiere of Mendelssohn's *Elijah*. Peter Cornelius (1824-1874), German composer of the popular opera *The Barber of Baghdad* and close friend of Liszt and Wagner, was also a prolific master of musical miniatures, as witness the unforgettable **The Three Kings**.

The most popular of all Christmas carols, **O Come, All Ye Faithful**, began life as the Latin hymn *Adeste Fideles*, the original text being attributed to John Wade. The music by John Reading didn't emerge until around 1720 and it was not until 1841 that the Reverend Frederick Oakley produced the familiar English translation that resounds around churches everywhere at Christmas time today.

The tune we all recognise as **Hark! The Herald Angels Sing** was composed by none other than Felix Mendelssohn – but not for this hymn! The text was written by Charles Wesley in 1739 to a sombre melody, and over a century later Englishman William Cummings had the inspired idea of resetting the words to a Mendelssohn tune composed originally in celebration of the printing press!

Ding Dong! Merrily on High is a traditional French carol which started life as a 16th-century folk dance that, when it was first published, was accompanied by instructions for it to be danced 'by lackeys and serving wenches'. The text that is sung today was written by George Ratcliffe Woodward, who makes the most of the onomatopoeic 'Ding dong' in his music, and sets the long descending melisma at the end to a drawn-out 'Gloria'.

The original melody of **In Dulci Jubilo** is thought to date from the 14th century, and since then has existed in many forms. It is a 'macaronic' carol, which uses a mixture of Latin and vernacular text. The basis for Pearsall's setting can be traced back to a Protestant service book from the year 1570, where it was called 'A very ancient song for Christmas Eve'.

The Holly and the Ivy dates back over 1000 years and was traditionally intended by pagans to be sung indoors in the hope that it might protect them as effectively as the resilient holly and ivy. It is from this song that the two popular colours associated with Christmas – red and green – were originally derived.

O Little Town of Bethlehem, memorably arranged here by the great English composer Ralph Vaughan Williams, was the combined effort of Philadelphian rector Phillip Brooks (who wrote the words) and his church organist Lewis Redner (1831-1908), after viewing Bethlehem at night from the hills of Palestine. In 1916 Vaughan Williams' close friend Gustav Holst, composer of *The Planets Suite*, made his haunting transcription of **Personent Hodie**, a German carol dating from the 14th century, closely associated with the Feast of the Holy Innocents on December 28th, which commemorates the children murdered by Herod in his vain attempt to kill the baby Jesus.

The words of **Past Three a Clock** were written by George Ratcliffe Woodward (who was also responsible for *Ding Dong! Merrily on High*), but the music can be dated back as far as the 17th century when it was linked with the waits, the original guilds of town pipers. Arranger Charles Wood (1866-1926), professor of music at Cambridge from 1924, also made a popular adaptation of **Shepherds in the Fields Abiding**, a traditional French carol dating from the 16th century.

Gabriel's message ('The angel from heaven came') is another ancient folk setting, emanating from the Basque region of France, which describes the Annunciation to the Virgin Mary as related in the New Testament (Luke, Chapter 1). The haunting **Coventry Carol** is another Biblical setting focusing on King Herod's imminent slaughter of the Innocents following Jesus' birth. Its composer remains a mystery, but we have John Stainer (of Crucifixion fame) to thank for rescuing it from oblivion during the late 1800s. The words to **While Shepherds Watched Their Flocks** were written in 1703 by Nahum Tate, Poet Laureate during the reign of Queen Anne. Originally set to a melody borrowed from Handel's opera Siroe (1728), it is more familiarly heard today via a Christopher Tye tune known popularly as 'Winchester Old'.

Away in a Manger was composed as recently as 1895 by Pennsylvanian William James Kirkpatrick (ironically the Americans tend to use the tune by James R Murray). **Rocking** ('Little Jesus, sweetly sleep') is the most popular of all Czechoslovakian carols whose swaying rhythms derive from the German custom of rocking children gently to sleep.

There are four more immensely popular carols, all of British origin: **See Amid the Winter's Snow** is the most famous piece by Sir John Goss (1800-188), organist at St. Paul's Cathedral from 1838 and teacher of Sir Arthur Sullivan; **God Rest You Merry, Gentlemen** was originally sung to the gentry by the town watchmen to earn additional money during the Christmas season. **The Sussex Carol** was discovered and written down by Ralph Vaughan Williams and Cecil Sharp, as sung by one Harriet Verrall of Monk's Gate, Sussex. **The First Nowell** is an English carol dating back to the 16th century but not published until 1833.

ONCE IN ROYAL DAVID'S CITY

Words by Cecil Frances Alexander
Music by H. J. Gauntlett

1. Once in roy - al Da - vid's ci - ty Stood a low - ly cat - tle shed,
2. He came down to earth from hea - ven Who is God and Lord of all,

Where a mo - ther laid her ba - by In a man - ger for his bed:
And his shel - ter was a sta - ble, And his cra - dle was a stall;

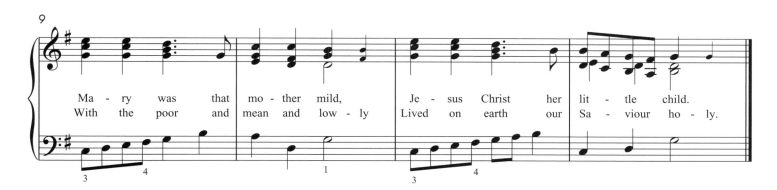

Ma - ry was that mo - ther mild, Je - sus Christ her lit - tle child.
With the poor and mean and low - ly Lived on earth our Sa - viour ho - ly.

3. And through all his wondrous childhood
He would honour and obey,
Love and watch the lowly maiden
In whose gentle arms he lay:
Christian children all must be
Mild, obedient, good as he.

4. For he is our childhood's pattern,
Day by day like us he grew,
He was little, weak, and helpless,
Tears and smiles like us he knew:
And he feeleth for our sadness,
And he shareth in our gladness.

5. And our eyes at last shall see him,
Through his own redeeming love,
For that child, so dear and gentle
Is our Lord in heaven above;
And he leads his children on
To the place where he is gone.

6. Not in that poor lowly stable,
With the oxen standing by,
We shall see him; but in heaven,
Set at God's right hand on high;
When like stars his children crowned
All in white shall wait around.

IN DULCI JUBILO

Traditional

THE HOLLY AND THE IVY

Traditional

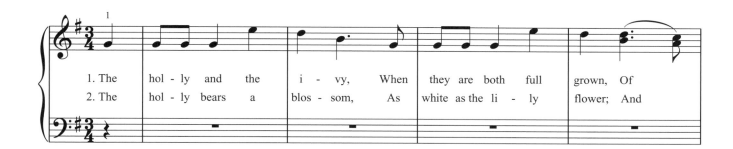

1. The hol - ly and the i - vy, When they are both full grown, Of
2. The hol - ly bears a blos - som, As white as the li - ly flower; And

all the trees that are in the wood, The hol - ly bears the crown. O the
Ma - ry bore sweet Je - sus Christ, To be our sweet Sa - viour.

Chorus

ris - ing of the sun, And the run - ning of the deer, The

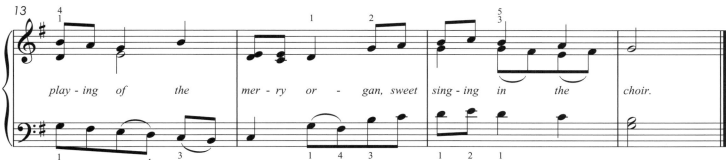

play - ing of the mer - ry or - gan, sweet sing - ing in the choir.

3. The holly bears a berry,
   As red as any blood;
   And Mary bore sweet Jesus Christ
   To do poor sinners good.

4. The holly bears a prickle,
   As sharp as any thorn,
   And Mary bore sweet Jesus Christ,
   On Christmas day in the morn.

5. The holly bears a bark,
   As bitter as any gall;
   And Mary bore sweet Jesus Christ,
   For to redeem us all.

6. The holly and the ivy
   When they are both full grown,
   Of all the trees that are in the wood,
   The holly bears the crown.

AWAY IN A MANGER

Words traditional
Music by William J. Kirkpatrick

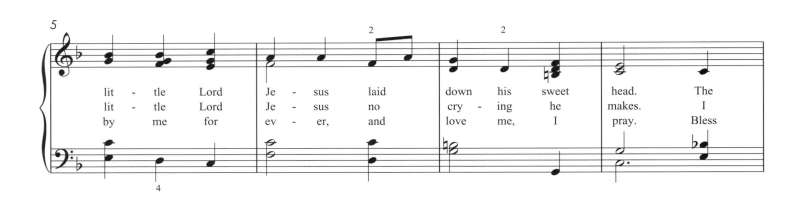

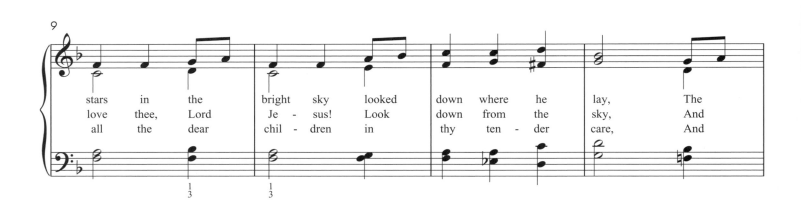

© 2009 by Faber Music Ltd

SEE AMID THE WINTER'S SNOW

Words by Edward Caswall
Music by John Goss

3. Say, ye holy shepherds, say
   What your joyful news today;
   Wherefore have ye left your sheep
   On the lonely mountain steep?

4. As we watch'd at dead of night,
   Lo, we saw a wondrous light;
   Angels singing,
   Told us of the Saviour's birth:

5. Sacred infant, all divine,
   What a tender love was thine,
   Thus to come from highest bliss
   Down to such a world as this:

6. Teach, O teach us, Holy Child,
   By thy face so meek and mild,
   Teach us to resemble thee,
   In thy sweet humility:

O LITTLE TOWN OF BETHLEHEM

Words by Phillips Brooks
Music traditional

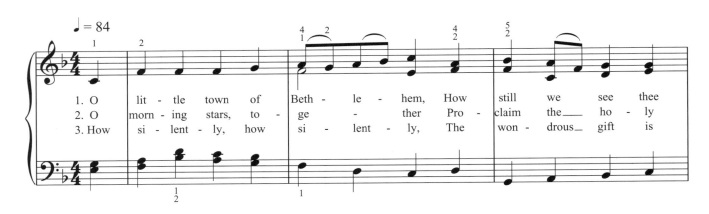

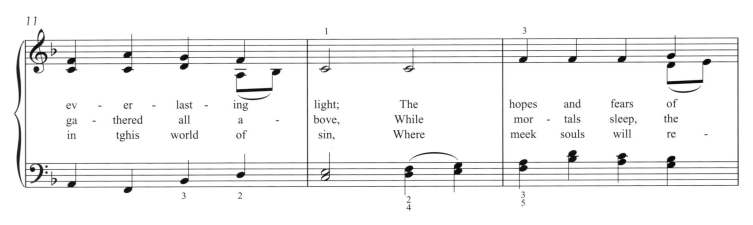

FOREST GREEN, music collected, adapted and arranged by Ralph Vaughan Williams (1872–1958)

GOD REST YOU MERRY, GENTLEMEN

Traditional

3. The shepherds at those tidings rejoiced much in mind,
   And left their flocks afeeding in the tempest, storm and wind,
   And went to Bethlehem straight-away this blessèd babe to find:
   O tidings . . .

4. But when to Bethlehem they came, whereat this infant lay,
   They found him in a manger where the oxen feed on hay;
   His mother Mary kneeling, unto the Lord did pray:
   O tidings . . .

SHEPHERDS IN THE FIELD ABIDING

Words by James Montgomery
Music traditional

3. Saints before the altar bending,
   Watching long in hope and fear,
   Suddenly the Lord, descending,
   In his temple shall appear:

4. Though an infant now we view him,
   He shall fill his Father's throne,
   Gather all the nations to him;
   Every knee shall then bow down:

PAST THREE A CLOCK

Words by G. R. Woodward
Music traditional

3. Mid earth rejoices
   Hearing such voices
   Ne'ertofore so well
   Carolling 'Nowell'.

4. Hinds o'er the pearly
   Dewy lawn early
   Seek the high stranger
   Laid in the manger.

5. Cheese from the dairy
   Bring they for Mary,
   And, not for money,
   Butter and honey.

6. Light out of star-land
   Leadeth from far land
   Princes, to meet him,
   Worship and greet him.

7. Myrrh from full coffer,
   Incense they offer:
   Nor is the golden
   Nugget withholden.

8. Thus they: I pray you,
   Up, sirs, nor stay you
   Till ye confess him
   Likewise, and bless him.

DING DONG! MERRILY ON HIGH

Words by George Ratcliffe Woodward
Music by Thoinot Arbeau

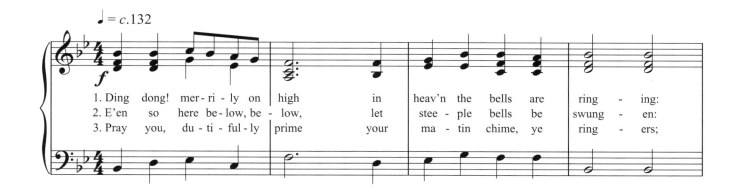

1. Ding dong! mer-ri-ly on high in heav'n the bells are ring - ing:
2. E'en so here be-low, be - low, let stee-ple bells be swung - en:
3. Pray you, du-ti-ful-ly prime your ma-tin chime, ye ring - ers;

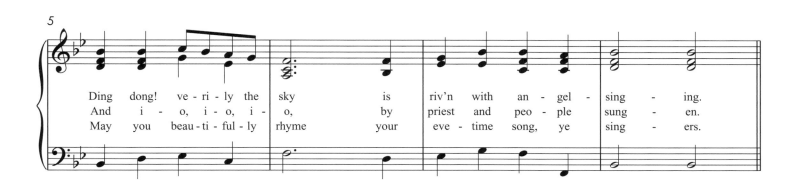

Ding dong! ve-ri-ly the sky is riv'n with an-gel-sing - ing.
And i - o, i - o, i - o, by priest and peo-ple sung - en.
May you beau-ti-ful-ly rhyme by your eve-time song, ye sing - ers.

Glo

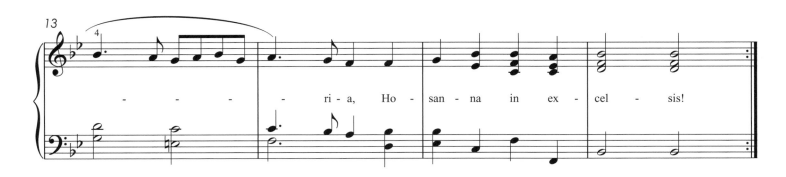

- - - ri-a, Ho-san-na in ex-cel - sis!

GABRIEL'S MESSAGE

Words by Sabine Baring-Gould
Music traditional

3. Then gentle Mary meekly bowed her head;
   'To me be as it pleaseth God,' she said.
   'My soul shall laud and magnify God's holy name.'
   Most highly favoured lady. Gloria!

4. Of her, Emmanuel, the Christ, was born
   In Bethlehem all on a Christmas morn,
   And Christian folk through-out the world will ever say:
   'Most highly favoured lady.' Gloria!

PERSONENT HODIE

Piae Cantiones, arr. Gustav Holst

3. Magi tres venerunt,
   Munera offerunt,
   Parvulum inquirunt,
   Stellulam sequendo,
   Ipsum adorando,
   Aurum, thus, thus, thus,
   Aurum, thus, thus, thus,
   Aurum, thus et myrrham
   Ei offerendo.

4. Omnes clericuli,
   Pariter pueri,
   Cantent ut angeli:
   'Advenisti mundo,
   Laudes tibi fundo.
   Ideo, o, o,
   Ideo, o, o,
   Ideo Gloria
   In excelsis Deo!'

SUSSEX CAROL

Traditional

1. On Christ - mas night all Chris - tians sing, To hear the news the an - gels bring. On Christ - mas night all Chris - tians sing To hear the news the an - gels bring. *News of great joy, news of great mirth, News of our mer - ci - ful King's birth.*

2. Then why should men on earth be so sad, Since our Re - deem - er made us glad, Then why should men on earth be so sad, Since our Re - deem - er made us glad, *When from our sin he set us free, All for to gain our li - ber - ty?*

3. When sin departs before his grace,
   Then life and health come in its place;
   When sin departs before his grace,
   Then life and health come in its place;
   Angels and men with joy may sing,
   All for to see the new-born King.

4. All out of darkness we have light,
   Which made the angels sing this night:
   All out of darkness we have light,
   Which made the angels sing this night:
   'Glory to God and peace to men,
   Now and for evermore. Amen.'

Collected and arranged by Ralph Vaughan Williams.
Reproduced by permission of Stainer & Bell Ltd, London, England. www.stainer.co.uk

COVENTRY CAROL

Traditional

THE THREE KINGS

Words and Music by Peter Cornelius
Translated by H.N. Bates
Arranged by Ivor Atkins

ROCKING

Words and Music Traditional
Translated by Percy Dearmer
Arranged by Martin Shaw

1. Lit - tle Je - sus, sweet - ly sleep, do not stir;
2. Ma - ry's lit - tle ba - by, sleep, sweet - ly sleep,

We will lend a coat of fur, We will rock you,
Sleep in com - fort, slum - ber deep; We will rock you,

rock you, rock you, We will rock you, rock you, rock you:
rock you, rock you, We will rock you, rock you, rock you:

See the fur to keep you warm, Snug - ly round your ti - ny form.
We will serve you all we can, Dar - ling, dar - ling lit - tle man.

WHILE SHEPHERDS WATCHED THEIR FLOCKS

Words attrib. Nahum Tate
Music traditional

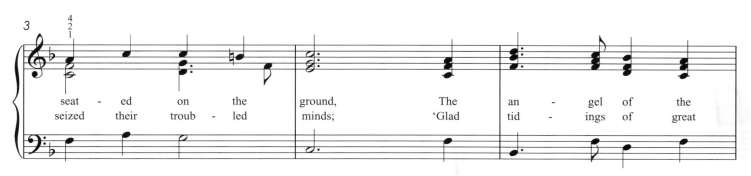

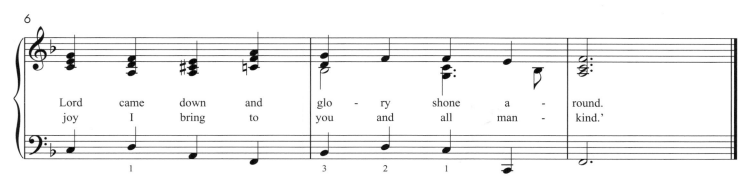

3. 'To you in David's town this day
Is born of David's line
A Saviour, who is Christ the Lord;
And this shall be the sign:

4. The heavenly babe you there shall find
To human view displayed,
All meanly wrapped in swathing bands
And in a manger laid.'

5. Thus spake the Seraph; and forthwith
Appeared a shining throng
Of angels praising God, who thus
Addressed their joyful song:

6. 'All glory be to God on high,
And on the earth be peace;
Goodwill henceforth from heaven to men
Begin and never cease.'

O COME, ALL YE FAITHFUL

Anon.

4. Lo! Star-led chieftains,
   Magi, Christ adoring,
   Offer him incense, gold and myrrh;
   We to the Christ Child
   Bring our hearts' oblations:

5. Child, for us sinners
   Poor and in the manger,
   Fain we embrace thee, with awe and love;
   Who would not love thee,
   Loving us so dearly?

THE FIRST NOWELL

Traditional

3. And by the light of that same star,
   Three wise men came from country far;
   To seek for a king was their intent,
   And to follow the star wherever it went:

4. This star drew nigh to the north-west;
   O'er Bethlehem it took its rest,
   And there it did both stop and stay
   Right over the place where Jesus lay:

5. Then enter'd in those wise men three,
   Full rev'rently upon their knee,
   And offer'd there in his presence
   Their gold and myrrh and frankincense:

6. Then let us all with one accord
   Sing praises to our heav'nly Lord,
   That hath made heav'n and earth of naught,
   And with his blood mankind hath bought.

HARK! THE HERALD ANGELS SING

Words by Charles Wesley
Music by Felix Mendelssohn

2. Christ, by highest heav'n adored,
Christ the everlasting Lord,
Late in time behold him come,
Offspring of a virgin's womb.
Veiled in flesh the Godhead see,
Hail th'incarnate Deity!
Pleased as man with man to dwell,
Jesus, our Emmanuel.
Hark! the herald angels sing
Glory to the new-born King.

3. Hail the heav'n-born Prince of Peace!
Hail the Sun of Righteousness!
Light and life to all he brings,
Ris'n with healing in his wings;
Mild, he lays his glory by,
Born that man no more may die,
Born to raise the sons of earth,
Born to give them second birth.
Hark! the herald angels sing
Glory to the new-born King.

The Chill With series
from Faber Music
each with a free Naxos CD

Adagio Chillout
Favourite slow movements and contemplative pieces,
including Beethoven's *Moonlight Sonata*,
Schumann's *Träumerei* and Mendelssohn's
Song without words 'Sweet Remembrance'.

0-571-52435-4

Chill with Chopin
Including masterpieces such as the *'Raindrop'* Prelude,
the *March Funèbre* from Sonata in B flat minor, and
the Waltz in A flat *'L'Adieu'*.

0-571-52438-9

Chill with Mozart
The most beautiful movements by Mozart,
including the first movement from Sonata in C K.545,
the Fantasia in D minor K.397 and
Adagio in B minor K.540.

0-571-52436-2

Chill with Debussy
Unmissable favourites such as *Clair de lune*,
La fille aux cheveux de lin and *Arabesque* No.1.

0-571-52437-0

To buy Faber Music publications or to find out about the full range of titles available
please contact your local music retailer or Faber Music sales enquiries:

Faber Music Ltd, Burnt Mill, Elizabeth Way, Harlow CM20 2HX
Tel: +44 (0) 1279 82 89 82   Fax: +44 (0) 1279 82 89 83
sales@fabermusic.com   fabermusic.com   expressprintmusic.com